Tomorrow

Other Books by Bradley Trevor Greive

The Blue Day Book
The Blue Day Journal and Directory
Dear Mom
Looking for Mr. Right
The Meaning of Life
The Incredible Truth About Motherhood
Priceless

Tomorrow

Adventures in an Uncertain World

BRADLEY TREVOR GREIVE

**Andrews McMeel
Publishing, LLC**

Kansas City

ISBN-13: 978-0-7407-5026-7
ISBN-10: 0-7407-5026-7

Library of Congress Catalog Control Number: 2003101104

Book design by Holly Camerlinck

Attention: Schools and Businesses

Andrews McMeel books are available at quantity discounts with bulk purchase for educational, business, or sales promotional use. For information, please write to: Special Sales Department, Andrews McMeel Publishing, 1130 Walnut Street, Kansas City, MO 64106.

Credits

Auscape International (www.auscape.com.au)
Austral International (www.australphoto.com.au)
Australian Picture Library
(www.australianpicturelibrary.com/au)
Bradley Trevor Greive (www.btgstudios.com)
Getty Images (www.gettyimages.com)
Photolibrary.com (www.photolibrary.com)
Stock Photos (www.stockphotos.com.au).

Detailed credit and contact details for the remarkable photographers whose work appears in *Tomorrow* and other books by Bradley Trevor Greive are freely available at www.btgstudios.com.

For Douglas Adams
1952–2001

A man who, in but a few short years, managed to fill the world with light and laughter, made the known universe a little bit bigger and a lot more interesting, waded through questions and malt whiskey that would bring tears to the eyes of mere mortals, and still found the time to climb Mount Kilimanjaro wearing a rhino costume.

Tomorrow

After long and thoughtful consideration,
I have come to a rather interesting conclusion.

Even though the global population is soaring into the billions, with thousands of religions, languages, philosophies, and cultures represented,

ultimately, there are only two kinds of people.

There are those who are certain the world is going
to hell in a handbasket,

and those who believe the best is yet to come.

(Actually, there is a third kind of person, who thinks
morris dancing is the highest form of creative expression,
but I *really* don't want to talk about them.)

Now, it hardly takes a genius to point out that we already live in dangerous and uncertain times. Why, all you have to do is turn on the TV, grab a copy of the newspaper,

or just take a look out your window.

It ain't a pretty sight.

Best friends and former allies

are suddenly tearing at each other's throats,

while unshakable economic powerhouses
are crashing to their knees on a daily basis.

You and I both know that good people get attacked in broad daylight all the time,

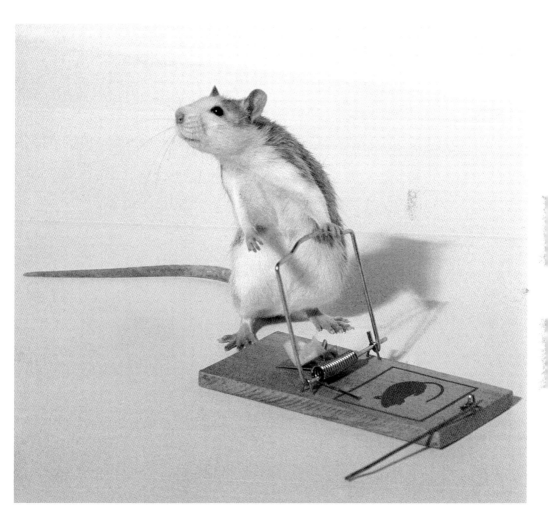

but somehow the bad guys never get caught.

It seems that everywhere you turn there are psychotic egomaniacs secretly trying to spoil your fun, drive you crazy, and generally make your life miserable.

Just for starters, there are shop assistants
with way too much attitude,

doughnuts with too much icing sugar,

unbearably long tap-dance routines in the middle
of your favourite old musicals,

and the dramatic after-effects of a
dangerously authentic vindaloo

that are made ten times worse because
public toilets never lock properly any more!

Of course, heartburn is nothing compared to heartache.
Even though we are frequently told there are
plenty of fish in the sea,

the truth is that most of us spend a great deal of our lives
physically and emotionally isolated, feeling utterly alone.

And if you do finally snuggle up to someone
who seems perfect for you,

you find out they snore so loudly
that your dreams need subtitles.

You just can't win!

If you listen to the professional doomsayers,
they will tell you that's barely the half of it.

They say these are our darkest days,
and the future looks bleaker than ever.

They tell us again and again that evil lurks everywhere—
in the streets, in the trees, in the media, in the air, in the water,
in the corridors of power, even in your sock drawer— 29

waiting impatiently to rise up when we least expect it
and sink its venomous teeth into our most tender regions.

And finally, they point out that at every office Christmas party there is always someone who feels compelled to do *this!*

"It's the end of the world," they shout. "It's all over!"

Now, what I find so confusing is that if these stone-faced folk truly believe all the scary stuff they preach, why do they choose to keep on living?

Okay, I freely admit that choking yourself to death
is not nearly as easy as it sounds,

and I was surprised to learn that you can't actually kill yourself simply by overdosing on bran fibre, although you certainly will become embarrassingly regular.

Luckily, thanks to modern technology, putting yourself out of
your misery has never been more convenient or affordable.

36

Of course, if life really appears that unpleasant and meaningless to you, go and see an eye specialist and then take a closer look. 37

You will find that there is always beauty and hope
in even the most awful circumstances.

There is always someone prepared to help those who ask.

There is always someone you can count on,

and there are a million special moments that can chase
the shadows from your face in an instant and will cost you
nothing but a few spare minutes.

Furthermore, romance is not dead.
In fact, there are actually more qualified tango instructors
working today than at any other time in history.

The odds of an unexpectedly intimate Jacuzzi encounter
have also never been better. 43

Although it may not be on your mind right now, the wisdom you glean from your joys and hardships can always be shared with someone else and, by doing so, you will leave the world a little better than when you found it.

Even though I think life is infinitely preferable to the alternative, I'm not pretending it's always easy or enjoyable. The truth is that sometimes life is so damned hard it gives you a cramp in your brain just thinking about what you have to do to make it through another twenty-four hours.

So it's no surprise that when they think about the future,
a lot of people feel anxious, somewhat depressed,
and generally confused and alarmed.

Even in the best of times there will never be a shortage of moaners and grumblers, but it's always fascinating to see how different people react during times of genuine uncertainty.

There are those who completely flip out
at the very first rumour of trouble

and start screaming, "The sky is falling, the sky is falling!"

But when you press them for hard evidence to explain their panic,
they admit they have nothing better to back up their position
than what "a little bird told them".

Somehow, it never occurs to them to wonder how credible
the little bird's source was in the first place.

Then there are the people who put on a big show about how they are not concerned in the least and know exactly

what to do about everything,

but when they are alone at night and the lights go out,
they may well be the most frightened of all.

There are also plenty of folk who are absolutely certain that the future is an extremely hostile place, no matter what you show or tell them. They stand ready to defend themselves from a million dangers every day,

until eventually they become as hard, ugly,
and cruel as the world they have imagined. 55

And finally, there are people who just want to dig an emotional bunker and jump inside. They think if they put up enough walls, they'll always be safe.

The irony is that instead of locking others out, they are actually locking themselves in. They may avoid a few things that make life difficult, but in the end, they also miss out on all the wonderful things that make life worth living,

and that makes about as much sense as
practising high fives on your own.

A far more reasonable approach is simply to put on
the bravest smile you've got

and admit that you are not the centre of the known universe. Therefore, there will always be things you don't know and can't control.

So when it's simply not your day and things get a little out of hand,
as they invariably do from time to time,

it's much more productive and far healthier to just sit back
and enjoy the absurdity of the moment.

This is not rocket science. It's just common sense that you should enjoy the bizarre fact that you live on a planet with at least six hundred unique flavours of ice cream,

instead of getting all worked up about the truly disgusting
taste of "atomic lemon sherbet with licorice ripple".

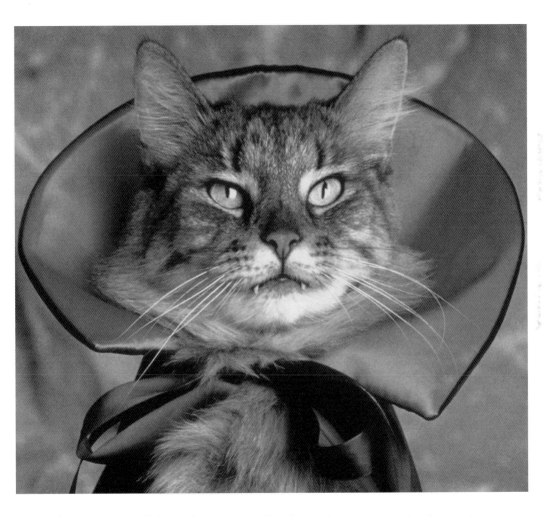

Likewise, it's definitely not worth obsessing about the intentions of all the sinister individuals who stalk the earth.

When it comes to ne'er-do-wells who betray and hurt others for their own personal gain, their wicked ways eventually catch up with them. They pretty much always get what they deserve in the end.

So in other words, a good support network is always valuable,
but hiring personal bodyguards is probably going too far!

Another reason why you shouldn't fear tomorrow is that
although you probably aren't what you eat,
you certainly are what you love.

This means that who you really are is always
accurately reflected in everything around you that is dear to
your heart—your close friends being one obvious example.

In this sense, it is fair to say that the world around you is a mirror.
Therefore you have a lot more control over the future
than you might think, because you can shape your world
just by being true to what you really care about.

Perhaps this will make sense to you, and then again, perhaps it won't.
You might say, "Aha! But how do you explain all the terrible things
in my world that I don't want?" That is certainly a valid question, 71

and my answer is, irritatingly enough, yet another question:
"What is it that you truly want?"

You see, it's what we truly want and love that influences
the world around us, whether we admit it or not.
For example, we often say we just want to be happy,

when what we mean is we want money—lots of it.

We say we want spiritual enlightenment and a
higher sense of understanding,

but what we really want are easy answers.

We say that we want love, affection, and companionship, 77

but what we really want is wild, passionate sex.

We say we just want to be accepted for who we really are,

when we really wish we were a little more glamorous

and had slimmer, firmer thighs.

As a rather wise person once said, "You can't fool Mother Nature."
There are certain immutable truths in this world that
you just can't talk your way out of.

Gravity will always get you down,

Belgian chocolates will go straight to your hips,

and sticking your finger in the toaster when your
crumpets are ablaze is always something you'll regret.

Likewise, you must be very careful what you wish for, because you simply cannot lie to yourself and get away with it. When you are not honest about what you want in life, you hurt those closest to you and yourself most of all.

Think very clearly about what you care most about. What is it that gets you excited about being alive? What do you really want to do with the limited time that you have? What will your personal legacy be?

But don't spend all your time dreaming about the future,
because the key to tomorrow is today.

No matter what brilliant answers you have for life's important questions,
ultimately what counts is that you break through the fears
and doubts that hold you back, and take action.

Be your own cheerleader.

Do something you never thought you'd ever do—
live in the moment.

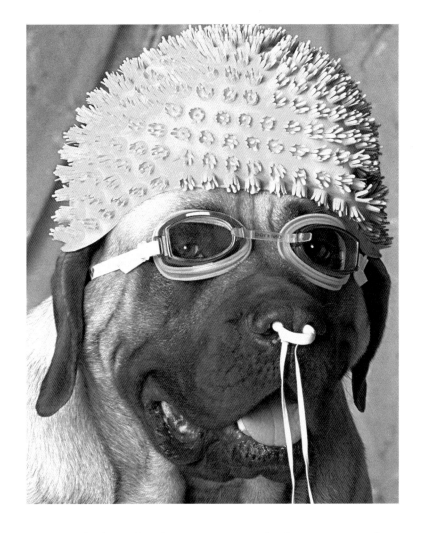

Keep in mind, though, that someone else's greatest adventure

could turn out to be your greatest nightmare.

So follow only your own road, wherever it leads you,
one step at a time.

Your journey through life is not a race or a competition, nor is it a boring highway without exits that you must trudge along for eternity.

Embrace the unpredictable and go exploring
for things that inspire you.

Take time out to enjoy the view.

The fact is that one day, instead of waking up for breakfast,
you will find yourself drawn down a long, dark tunnel toward a bright
and beautiful light, and your journey will have come to an end.

In that moment, when your entire life passes by before your eyes, I really don't think you will care too much about the amount of money you made, the frequent-flyer miles you accrued, the awards you won, the car you owned, the value of your stock, or the number of times you got your picture in the newspaper.

Instead, I believe the most important things in your life will
probably be the smooches you shared,

the nights you spent gazing in wonder at the stars,

all the funny-looking snow angels you made,

the first drops of summer rain caught on your tongue,

104   and the time that someone special whispered, "I love you."

Don't waste the present worrying about the future.
It will come soon enough—I promise.

In the meantime, I suggest you keep your chin up,
put your walking shoes on,

and follow your heart to the ends of the earth.

As you make this journey, always remember that
each day is a precious gift. If you can enjoy it
for what it is and make the most of it,

then believe it or not, there is another
extraordinary gift waiting for you.

Tomorrow.

Acknowledgments

These days I often find myself wondering how so few words could have taken me so far or propelled me into such glittering company. When I look in the mirror, I see only a slightly shop-soiled Tasmanian and not much else. Yet because I have been blessed with the support of my incredible team at BTG Studios along with the wit and wisdom of publishing luminaries such as Christine Schillig at Andrews McMeel (U.S.A.) and Jane Palfreyman at Random House (Australia), I have been able to accomplish far more than I ever dreamed possible. To these fabulous folk, as well as the passionate publishers and beloved readers throughout the globe who have believed in and enjoyed my humble endeavours, I offer my eternal heartfelt thanks.

As always, I must emphasize that my little books would be nothing without the superb photographs that drive the visual narrative from beginning to end, and I encourage everyone to celebrate these artists and the photo libraries that have contributed to this book by seeking out their contact details posted at www.btgstudios.com.

Finally, I must admit that this book was wholly inspired by the remarkable adventures of my international literary agent and fencing coach, Albert J. Zuckerman of Writers House New York, which took place during a creative work-shop/ice-fishing trip in Alaska during the winter of 1967. According to the version shared with me by Professor Stephen Hawking (another Writers House